The Prince of Wails

Stephen Knight's two previous collections, *Flowering Limbs* (1993) and *Dream City Cinema* (1996), were both shortlisted for the T. S. Eliot Prize. His novel *Mr Schnitzel* (2000) won the Arts Council of Wales Book of the Year Award. Born in Swansea, he now lives in London.

From reviews of *Dream City Cinema*:

'Knight's is an urban world, edgy and strangely lit, at its most vivid when described in the echoey full rhyme that he handles so well.' – Helen Dunmore, *Observer*

'A masterpiece in miniature, packed with surprisingly enthusiastic and musical treatments of entropy, whether universal or personal, by a top craftsman with a quirky and disconcertingly loveable voice.' – Robert Potts, *Guardian* (Books of the Decade)

also by Stephen Knight

POETRY

Flowering Limbs (Bloodaxe, 1993)
The Sandfields Baudelaire (Smith/Doorstop, 1996)
Dream City Cinema (Bloodaxe, 1996)

FICTION

Mr Schnitzel (Penguin, 2000)

FOR CHILDREN

Sardines and other poems (Macmillan, 2004)

AS EDITOR

I am twenty people! A third anthology from The Poetry School
(with Mimi Khalvati; Enitharmon, 2007)

THE PRINCE OF WAILS

Stephen Knight

CB editions

First published in 2012
by CB editions
146 Percy Road London W12 9QL
www.cbeditions.com

Printed in England by Blissetts, London W3 8DH

ISBN 978-0-9567359-6-6

for Ted

Dad somehow meets my daughter
when she is tall and he is back
in the garden of the house where I was born.
Side by side and still above the water
shining in the goldfish pond, they look
for what? A tail? Two eyes? A face
neither would be able to discern
now afternoon is changing into night?

The surface of the pond is black.
What happened to the time?
Did I turn
to register an alteration of the light
then drop at my feet that bedtime book
I was reading aloud, into space?

Acknowledgements

Times Literary Supplement, *text* (Germany), *Poetry Wales*, *Poetry Review*, *Poetry London*, *Planet*, *Пламък* (Bulgaria), *Oxford Poetry*, *The North*, *New Welsh Review*, *Mississippi Review*, *London Review of Books*, *The Literary Review* (US), BBC Radio 4, *Poetry Wales: 40 Years* (Seren, 2005), *Oxygen: New Poets from Wales* (Seren, 2000), *The Forward Book of Poetry 2006* (Forward/Faber, 2005), *Coastline* (Gwasg Carreg Gwalch, 2006), The British Council's *New Writing 10* (Picador, 2001) and *The Art of Life* (Lawrence & Wishart, 2000).

'Happly Ever After' won a small prize in the 2010 *TLS* Poetry Competition.

Commissioned by Lavinia Greenlaw for *Signs and Humours: The Poetry of Medicine* (Calouste Gulbenkian Foundation, 2007), 'The Nightingale Standard' is constructed from material found in *The Family Physician* (The Caxton Publishing Company, 1951).

An earlier version of the poem in boustrophedon was commissioned by Jude Winnan and broadcast in 1998 by BBC2 Wales on Swansea Night.

'Our Father' responds to a poem of the same title by Alan Perry.

Thanks to Paul Henry, Daljit Nagra and Oliver Reynolds for their advice; to my brother for the ubi sunt; to my daughter for her orthography; and to Kate Knight, these poems' first reader.

Contents

Thank You for Having Me 3
A British Summer 4
The Nightingale Standard 5
Benthills Notebook 8
Methuselah 10
What with the Rain 11
Tour through the Whole Island of Me 12
The Cure for Snow 14
Old Man Up a Tree 15
So Early in the Year 16
The Gods 18
Album 19
Mythologies 20
Fifty Second Life 22
Our Father 23
Walter de la Mare 24
A Book of Hours 26
The House Where We Were Born 27
EVERYTHING MUST GO! 28
The Summer of Love 29
The Land of Nod 30
Butterfly 32
A Tick-Box Life 33
Why You Cannot Go Downstairs 36
The Smiles 38
The End of Mumbles Pier 40

On Turning Fifty 42
An ABC of Winter 44
The Light Programme 46
Lost Things 47
We Lived Here 48
Happy Ever After 49

99 Poems 51

The Prince of Wails

Thank You for Having Me

everyone's packing up everyone's going home
the girl guides and the traffic wardens all the souls
the neighbourhood has harboured downing placards
turning signs like *PUKKA-PIES . . . they're delicious* CLOSED
CLOSED EVERYTHING MUST GO the dummies stripped of clothes
don't mourn them uselessly [something something something]
men whose shoulders sink a little further from their ears
hail cabs or wait for buses Dora *¡vãmonos!*
The Ink Spots old poor Johnnie Ray The Prince of Wails
The Nabob of Sob running like a younger man
the boy in fluffy slippers and the men on stilts
lolloping past the locksmiths outside New Cross station
HARRY & SON established 1960 now
where are you Harry everyone's going home
it's raining in this poem here come on let's shelter
underneath these rough-and-tumble alexandrines
yonder raindrops dripping off an overhanging word
shaken from umbrellas under awnings *allons-y*
the pink girl in the boob tube in the first class carriage
insects from the cracks in paving stones conquistadores
in tarnished [technical term for piece of armour]
bankers vendors Captain Cook home before it's dark
before the lights are necessary in houses where the chairs
hold out their puffy/threadbare arms to take them in
everyone's leaving clickdripclickdropclickdripclickdrop
so many footsteps now or shadows rounding corners
bone-dry box-shaped holes in car parks everywhere

we have to go home in the end leave the swings
to hang their heads strap you in then steer you back
through the high tide's twigs and plastic see the river
cross that road we took not long ago

A British Summer

My boredom chock-a-block
with furniture – the desk
in bits, the sofa cushions
cluttering the bed, drawers
shoved beneath the dresser
– I stare at Wimbledon
while listening to the man
restretch then clean
the carpets in two rooms.
Suds rumbling in their drum,
the smell of pine detergent
creeping up to me.

Two hours of plucky Brits,
mauve clouds, the covers on,
or grim-faced teenagers
washed up before their spots
have cleared, then I descend
like Norma Desmond,
out of touch, magnanimous;
and all the little dents
where chairs and tables stood
have disappeared, as though
the years of being here
had never happened.

The Nightingale Standard

A sick person who fears his nurse or who knows that her handling of him will cause him pain [. . .] is liable to get nervous and morbid.
– *The Family Physician*, 1951

An ideal sickroom, facing west:
Ornaments and useless furnishings dispensed with,
Dusted, disinfected pictures on the wall,
Drugs placed carefully in drawers,
Light literature,
My correspondence littering the floor,
Damp dusters for the woodwork,
Beef tea, soon.

Now, I'm drinking cocoa from the nibs.
Clear, like coffee, and most refreshing. Refreshing me.
Wine whey? Milk tea? Egg flip?
– Please. Anything but cocoa from the nibs.

Business-like in rubber heels, methodical,
Nurse contemplates the muscles of my face.

Air hunger
Air passages, obstruction of
Alkalis
Allotments
Amputation
Anvil bone

Stewed according to size and age,
Stewed pigeon next. The trussing string
Removed, it's almost free from grease.
Broiled chops? Stewed sweetbread? Tripe?
– All right. This bird is not restoring me.

18 breaths a minute, 15 when I'm old.

A regular exchange of air:
The bottom sash raised every day;
At night, the top 3 inches.

A slight touch here, the smoothing of a wrinkle there.
The under mackintosh pulled straight.
I ruffle my covers, adopt all sorts of attitudes.
(A benefit, both mentally and physically.)

Business-like in rubber heels, methodical,
Nurse

- keeps back the crowd
- lays, around my bed, linoleum
- dashes water on my face
- applies a little powdered starch
- encourages the bleeding
- gives me ice to suck

Lathered, several times a day, with tarry soap,
I'm trussed from toe to head.

18 breaths a minute, 15 when I'm old.

Looking for the bottle labelled POISON,
Nurse shows her strength of character.
She has given me a sporting chance.

I have no foreign bodies in my feet.
I have no fish hook in my hand.

Russell viper
Rubber bandages
Robert Jones abduction frame
Roundworm
Rigor mortis
Rickety rosary
Reticulitis
Rescue me

Benthills Notebook

The House in the Clouds. The frozen windmill. Sizewell B.
A wooden house a stone's throw from the stony sea.
Five beds with twelve pillows, and every one
hard as the shore and the light of the low, October sun.
A light left on on the landing, the bedroom door
left open all night. Precarious on the shaking floor,

the wardrobe shaking its hangers at me.

A walk in the northerly wind, or sitting inside –
before a single pane of frosted glass – watching the tide.
Deckchairs in a cupboard. The top of my head
brushing the lintels. No telephone and no TV; instead,
a borrowed radio. Light Vessel Automatic. A crusty stain.
The snug of The Dolphin gathering rain.

The North Sea dressed up like a bride,

cushions leaking foam. My shaver filling a metal bin.
The clocks put back, the evenings coming in
by half past four. Anglers camped out on the beach
all night. Flatfish staying out of reach.
My notebooks full of rubbish – metaphors
emptier than all my eight rooms' empty drawers;

a haiku I couldn't begin.

Perfecting a conjuring trick, the sea draws back its hand
from time to time to show me sand.
More furniture than floor. Walking the pebbly shelf,
a man with a metal detector keeps himself
to himself. Long shadows for much of the day
then the lighthouse throwing its light away.

Big sky. The Long Wave band.

Methuselah

Another box of cornflakes
Another sunny day

Another plastic toy
To throw away

What with the Rain

shaking the door
and the bad tree
(hammering down!)

a mug of tea
on the sill, a brown
apple core

and the dustbin
gone for ever,
lost in a blur

I could never
have hoped to hear
you walking in

but now you are,
it seems, to see
my wasted day

and I'm not ready
to hear you say
just how far

you've come for me;
your cold hand
on my shoulder.

Tour through the Whole Island of Me

I was Spider-Man
2-faced shifty stuck to walls
who listens to the boy with hairy hands?
cue zither
I was Orson Welles
looking on the ants
I was Charlie Farnsbarns
without the hoopy jumper
and with very little in the way of Menace
I was Dennis
I was Laurel
boo-hoo
I was William Wordsworth
slopey-shouldered on the hills and cliffs
but sick of daffodils
La vita non è sogno
I was Quasimodo
the one who wrote no poetry
uh-oh
I was Mersault
patricidal matricidal harmless on the beach
albeit dressed in black
I was The Man Who Never Was
lounging on the sand
I was Gary Sprake
fumbling the back pass
hanging from the big hand
I was Harold Lloyd
I was Roger Waters
looking out to sea

I was Rod McKuen
    the one who wrote no poetry
    a smaller head and fewer strings
I was all 5 Thunderbirds
I was Armstrong
    bobbing on the moon
I was Billy Liar
    being someone unlike me
I was Leon Trotsky
    con paracetamols
    with neither wives nor palaces
I was that Iraqi potentate
    lead me out
    you've seen what I'm about
    yep?
        yup
    yee-haw! I'm fuckin' guilty
    string me up!
I was Kafka
I was Edgar Al *and* Po
    without the girls and parishes
I was neither of the Thomases
I was Alfred Tennyson
    looking out to sea
    away down the river
I was Robert Louis Stevenson
    bring my boats ashore boys
I was Spider-Man

The Cure for Snow

for my father

We need a cure for snow:
A level tablespoon,
One jab to make the winter go.
We need a panacea soon
– Something for pain –

Perhaps a doctor to explain
Low cloud away,
A tonic for the rain
Washing over Langland Bay,
An ointment to apply to fog,

Inhalers, creams and pills
To combat hail and sleet
Or medicine that kills
Black ice on every street.
Something painless, please,

Something strong to ease
The squalls, to calm
The shaking of the trees
– Their naked arms,
Their hollowed hearts.

Old Man Up a Tree

High in the oak, that geezer
who stares across the bay
towards Port Talbot steelworks
    is there again today

in his tatty uniform:
putties stream from his feet,
his service cap is holey,
    his webbing incomplete.

Now and then, he turns inland
to men in flowered shirts
with hair below their collars,
    to birds in mini-skirts

who wave – and so he chuckles,
begins another song
about his bollocks, then shouts
    'I WON'T BE HERE FOR LONG'

What's become of his ladder?
He's far too frail to climb
so much as a flight of stairs.
    I will ask him some time.

But now, expecting spring,
he drags on one cigarette
after another; perishing,
    oh, and very wet.

So Early in the Year

Presumably the whole point is that there should be no continuum:
of anything. That failures of memory are but a proof of a living organism's
subordination to the laws of nature. No life is meant to be preserved.
– Joseph Brodsky, *In a Room and a Half*

'I really ought to stop
climbing trees,' you said,
nipping the filter off
another low-tar cigarette
then settling your arm
lightly on my shoulder,
giving me a squeeze
as if you didn't know
you were dead.

– THUMP THUMP
thumpthumpthump . . .
The builder opposite
plays Capital all day.
His hammer in the air,
a nail between his teeth,
he dances,
dances like a little boy
till everything's OK.

The Green, fluorescent
after rain, is buzzing,
with ZIPPO'S grimy
Day-Glo trailers
scattered like toys.
While men lug rope,
funambulists in tights

pitch in, or practise
death-defying feats.

You looked quite wrong –
your eyes too far apart,
your hair too long
and coppery – and yet
the way in dreams
we know, Joseph, I knew
(deep down) that it
was you, knee-deep
in reams of leaves.

The golden chain tree's
flowers blew away
so early in the year,
now wizened seedpods
hang above the path,
but they're juggling fire
out there, balancing –
on long broom-handles
– children, who throw

their arms out wide.

The Gods

              wear woollens all year round,
brandish plastic-coated bus-passes
everywhere, & lose their glasses
(broken glasses someone's bound
with sticky tape) once every day.

Their faces crack. Their marble ears
lie, snapped off, in the grass for years.
The years are wearing them away.

We say 'YOU'RE LOOKING WELL'
& yet an overcrowded shop
can frighten them
                              – so, with a mile
to go before they reach their stop
they rise, wobbling in the aisle

to ring & ring the bell.

Album

William, Gladys and Edward Knight. Where are they standing?
William, Gladys and Edward Knight. Where are they camping?
Do you know the name of the school?
Roy Woods and Edward Knight but where are they?
Where are they?
This looks like London Zoo. Who is the person in the middle?
Who is the person 3rd from the left? Where are they?
Who are the boys either side of Edward Knight? Where are they?
Who is the boy in the picture?
Who are the two with Edward Knight?
Where?
Where is this?
Where is this? Who is the small boy?
I can recognise Gladys, Edward and Sam but who are the others?
Where is he?
Same as above
Same as above
Embankment London
Who is the woman on the left?
Gladys and Edward Knight. Where are they?
Who are the two on the right?
Are you sure they are Sam and Edward Knight?
Who is in the sidecar?

Mythologies

Notre passé est dans un ailleurs et une irréalité imprègne les lieux
et les temps. – Gaston Bachelard, *La Poétique de L'Espace*

My heart still in the scullery
Tucked in a drawer, but whither

- The sticks of ghostly furniture?
- The arras, plush with dust?
  (Behind which Mother hid,
  As mothers do ere long,
  If only from the dust)
- That open drawer of knives?
- My winning hand of hearts?
- Our headless ghost?

*

Down corridors our father hung
With dead Black Sheep then up, up –

The attic! where that working
Model of The Maginot Line
Ticked and tocked, all night
With Father's help.

The sheep that shuffled through
My head on sleepless nights
While Father paced the attic,
Modelling The Past.

*

That whisper from the cellar
Rising through the house
Could be my mother's steam iron
Heavy as a stone.

Outside, the empty tree
(The tree I used to climb)
Leans against the house.

Its leaves have filled the cellar
Where my mother used to iron.

My heart is made of stone.

Fifty Second Life

after Paul Ferris

His background, legend, restlessness;
indulgent mother; father's influence;

thieving; camping; enter Daniel Jones;
learns to drink; seeks 'philosophy';

rejection slips; 'gonorrhoea' episode;
embraced by Edith Sitwell;

flees creditors; wartime drinking;
synopsis for 'A Book of Streets';

in ruined Swansea; work stagnates;
meets Charlie Chaplin; sexual affairs;

sails home; his father's death;
treated by Dr Feltenstein; unhappy,

unwell; 'eighteen straight whiskies';
half a grain of morphine;

his effects; his memorial;
his posthumous affluence.

Our Father

Let's look once more, now
that it's dark – you and me –
let's dig holes in the sand

then peer inside, let the sea
fill them up while we stand
and watch, dressed anyhow.

(. . . Your ancient negligée.
My dressing gown, trailing
in rock pools half the night.)

By now we could be scaling
slippery cliffs, our torchlight
sweeping round the bay.

Keep warm inside the car –
but any of his bones I find
I keep. Try my coat for size,

or if you have to sit behind
the steering wheel, itemise
the things we have so far.

His car-rug, stiff with brine.
Our tartan Thermos flask
that rattles if it's shaken.

Walter de la Mare

a turgid and windy old 'saul.
– Philip Larkin, 1943

The study door is shut.
Five o'clock.
Beyond the leaded windows, dusk
Shaken from a tree
Like birds
When Walter de la Mare
Murmurs *knock, knock?*
– No one's there.

Days of 1954 outside.
Inside: Walter de la Mare.

A hallway's organza,
Taxidermy, lace, chinoiserie
And Walter de la Mare
Before his room at last,
Knocking the door.

Burton, Gibbon, Webster locked away.

In this light it's difficult to see
The undermaid
Whose pinafore's as white
As oh,
Let's say Napoleonic snow,
Her dress as crisp as night.
Trailing a finger
Down the panelled corridor
She slips from sight.

Jackdaws probe
A pyramid of leaves.
It's almost half past Life
Inside, but every lamp is cold.
Waiting at the door
Of Walter de la Mare,
Walter de la Mare –
Who does things differently
– Suspects
That, hidden in this stanza,
There has to be
A knife.

Elsewhere, in a draughty room,
The shade of Thomas Hardy
Stalks the wing-backed chairs.

Like ashes in a grate,
A whisper stirs
The unenlightened air.
Bells shake above the lintels
As Walter de la Mare
Leans towards his oak-faced door
To ask *Is anybody there?*

A Book of Hours

Snowflakes knock
knock knocking on the glass
but no one answering

and yet the bedside clock
allows the hours to pass

Grown-ups deep
in leather swollen chairs
lay books across their laps

while we are fast asleep
alone upstairs

Celestial light-bulbs burn
about their heads all night
and on till dawn

All night the pages turn
and every page is white

The House Where We Were Born

The furniture has shifted overnight:
the locks have changed: the pictures on the wall
appear the same, but no one there is us:
the lights shine incorrectly in the hall.

Whose cat is curled on someone else's lap
and who, at last, is answering the door
to someone stepping from an unlit road
that's nowhere we have occupied before?

The flowerbeds are fake. The fish are stone
inside their concrete bed. The apple tree
that did not live when we were living there
ticks in a steady wind; ticks steadily.

Why are the streets where no one's heard of us
so cold? And why do men loom into view
from nowhere, now and then? (Amnesiacs
who swear we look like someone we once knew.)

EVERYTHING MUST GO!

That afternoon the pavements shine
like glass   although it's pelting down/
it isn't raining any more

you leave the station of a town
you've never visited before
passing a taxi rank   a red sign

light-headed traffic on the avenue
of double yellow lines   elm trees
at last   coming into leaf

You cover your eyes and no one sees
the new taste in your mouth is grief/
is love   and no one speaks to you

Chained up outside a crumbling shop
a mongrel watches someone kiss
the window   point   then say

That to a woman mouthing *This?*
Or this?   and you are miles away
lost/waiting for the rain to stop

while   in the violet light   clean
paving-stones and golf umbrellas glow
(your own face something of a shock

reflected in the runny window
where the carriage clock
or the wedding ring had been)

The Summer of Love

                    of Patrick Troughton's puckish Dr Who
of the dark-wood-and-mullion-doored bureau

and the coal bunker dwarfed by my father's shed
of my canary-yellow candlewick bedspread

of the dog at our back door waiting for bones
(its hind leg broken on Pentregethin Rd)

of the day my father's mother died
downstairs
                    of the day my father turned aside

of the walnut sideboard I hid my toys beneath
of the snails that clung to our pond's greasy slopes

of the garage my father refused to complete
of the space where a door should have been

The Land of Nod

The sea would make us watch its fall and rise
days whole   eyes the in channel the looked we
slid by   the long waves dazzled as they hypnotised
hand the by fathers our took we when and
like tugs they turned so slowly in our wake
palm our in water of weight its   cars bumper red
the wide eyed goldfish   then the helter skelter
time any at come could shout the then and
to leave the land and give ourselves to water
arms their in rocking waves   gifts like wrapped
the boat and us   our faces under sheets of spray
channel the   sea fizzing the around blown voices our
climbed aboard to tuck us in   we rose and fell
wave upon wave   wave after wave
when gift shops let their shutters down
harbour's nodding the   sails like asleep curled we
cold face frowning as we passed
never which *ship this upon blessing thy pour*
dreamt the waves would go so far to ruin it
old in rot the stem to attempts despite it ruin
arthritic bones   in paint which bubbles then unfolds
tar of sheets with work its done had sea the
oil and salt   so *pour thy blessing upon this ship*
men blind like beach the across move then
listening for signals   those things the water
underfoot somewhere were coast our round pushes
forgotten rusty things the sea locks tightly in
shut smooth waves the sand of chest a
called to us   we moved like archaeologists
water to ourselves gave shivering wrapped gift
and in return the water gave us solitude

fish eyed wide mouthed open   fish and
slithered from our fists like bits of autumn light
hull the on knocking waves   gulls of cloud a
wave after wave   wave upon wave
    us with done had sea the when and
we dwindled to a night light on the long
horizon

Butterfly

My father came back, in the early morning, for a swim.
When the bath was full of cold, cold water he swam
a length or two and I sat there watching him
manoeuvre like a dolphin. I was happier than I am.

He was agile in that narrow space, and strong.
His skin was taut again, his forearms shone.
Much longer than it ever was in life, his hair was long
and curly, reaching to his waist.
Then he was gone –

A Tick-Box Life

1 Are the following foolish, or
merely out of reach?

☐ A 28-inch waist
☐ A face like the one I had
☐ *A la recherche du temps*
perdu instead of *The Beach*

2 Is a purposeless existence
making you sad?
If nothing else presents itself,
you can always . . .

☐ Teach

3 A walk across the lawn,
towards

☐ My potting shed
☐ A motorbike
☐ No Particular Place Go

with my head in my hands/
my hands on my head.

4 Difficulties with

- ☐ Loctite®
- ☐ Women
- ☐ God

then, uh-oh.

5 TV, or

- ☐ A Book at Bedtime
- ☐ Tablets

instead.

6 Hilarious gaffes with

- ☐ Anniversaries
- ☐ Tickets
- ☐ A nappy

7 Writing as if I were

- ☐ Disaffected
- ☐ Distressed
- ☐ Incompetent

when, in fact, I'm happy.
(If happy's being happy
being like the rest.)

8 My career to date?

- ☐ Promising
- ☐ Fortunate
- ☐ Crappy

9 Can

- ☐ DIY skills
- ☐ Money
- ☐ Worship

make me strong?

10 Should I keep this
from you, until you're

- ☐ 18?
- ☐ Married?
- ☐ Past caring?

and will you
get me wrong?

11 What were the reasons?
What can this possibly mean?
The nearest I could manage to

- ☐ An apology?
- ☐ A song?

Why You Cannot Go Downstairs

Because it's early.
Because it's dark.
Because the cat is sleeping on her chair.
Because it's rude
    to wake next door before the sun.
Because it's cold.
Because the wind and rain intrude
    wherever they can, to leave their mark
    here and there.
Because you should still be asleep.
Because men and women work below,
    moving sticks of furniture for fun.
    (Listen. You can hear them creep
    about our rain-soaked rooms then go
    the way they come.)
Because the clocks
    need rest as well.
Because your toys
    are curiously terrible things
    before it's light.
Because of noise –
    talking books, mechanical wings
    flapping like mad in your toy box,
    footsteps, laughter.
    Yes, even that.
Because it's night.
Because.
Because we're in a state.
Because it's sleep we're after
    not electric light.

Because it's early /
because it's late.
  Either way,
  don't leave us yet.

The Smiles

erupt one day from nothing ah November yes and yellowed woodwork
pleading for a lick of paint and smiles escape despite the bleedin' rain

in spite of dirty dirty windows letting in so little dirty light
and never mind the door ajar forget the keys there go the smiles

a smile on Staines Road legging it before we take advice upending
bins another scrapes a stick along the Blucher's ruby frontage

now which way the smiles might go um north who knows or west
towards my mother's face (nah) east a hearse parked up one smile

flickers in the rear view mirror oh as if the shade of Stanley Spencer
stretched sat up then said *hello* a smile surveys the checkouts

2–4–1 a bingo smile ascends the cheeks of Mrs Y but nothing now
can stop the smiles no barricades no glyphosates no photographs

of R. S. Thomas no nor e'en Sir Geoffrey Hill a wingèd smile
arising like a prayer above the A316 heading for the coast

it isn't you and then PARP ting another smile strikes up its instruments
BONG CLANG a Swanee whistle smile kazoos and triangles *it's me*

a smile will not negotiate come down remove its Batman costume ever
does not care about the traffic jam the cries of *JUMP* and *HURRY UP*

smiles eructating everywhere no symptoms nothing curable
nothing in a test tube nothing lumpy no and nothing with a hole

one smile breaks over Feltham sending down a swizzle stick of light
to light Eduard who stops and lo a smile curls round his cigarette

a smile is spraying words on trains a slide a climbing frame a swing
a smile recycles bottles trees undress because it's cold a smile looks

puddles in the eye and God looks back a four-leafed smile plays
Dexys thirty years too late a smile remembers then a smile runs

sopping flags up flagpoles checks its watch decides to carry on
a smile reverses in a space too small for smiles a smile calls back

a smile avoids the cracks a smile stooping for a penny finds a pound
a smile agrees a smile is at the door and someone lets it in

The End of Mumbles Pier

The pressure drops.
– Missing the sun
bay-fronted shops
on Bryn-y-Môr Rd
shut, one by one.
The day's forgotten
fruit goes rotten.
Yawns explode.

That stuff the sea
packs tightly in
a chest of sand
. . . perpetually
and anyhow . . .
resurfaces now
as clouds begin
to cross the land.

– However slow
they are, days pass
and, every night,
looking for a ball
lost in long grass
thirty years ago,
the lighthouse light
finds nothing at all

along the coast
except for starfish
the waves discard –
giving up the ghost
until they're hard
enough to wish
upon – and then
the pier again.

My pockets are full
of pennies and sand.
A tugboat, I take
my daddy's hand.
I pull and I pull
because he turns so
slowly in my wake,
and won't let go.

On Turning Fifty

for my daughter

We could stay up late with Stanley Kunitz,
    Harry Patch, Bob Hope and Run Run Shaw
To watch an autumn evening fall to bits

    Then paint or crayon, gathered on the floor
As cosy as the streets are cold and coaly
    With every toy dismantled in its drawer,

And when we reach the time that's wholly
    Unfamiliar – 3 or 4 a.m. – yawning,
We could bet on who will roly-poly

    Down the hill and on till morning:
Harry? Stanley? Run Run? You, or me?
    Fizzy, we could giggle without warning,

Pray for biscuits, pop and cups of tea.
    You could mess with glue and glitter
And I could listen to the BBC

    While pipistrelles and whatnots flitter,
Fossicking for tasty, little things;
    Or I could make an origami critter

That flaps its head and folds its wings
    – A creature nothing ever wants to catch –
Then caterwaul when Bob Hope sings,

Or lean in close as close to Harry Patch
To hear him call me, softly, *chum* or *mate*,
And with our front door off the latch

We'll trust the sunrise to procrastinate
And every song-struck bird to wait . . .
So, Sylvie, shall we stay up late?

An ABC of Winter

for my son

They make the most of it,
    The crumbs of snow,
Decorating corners where
    The cold sheep go
For shelter, levelling
    The margins.
                Below,
Look! black waves
    Shatter on the sand.
It's quite a show.

Perhaps the winter has
    Our future planned
And means to cover
    Every scrap of land.
Unlike those sheep,
    My lad, I understand.
The wind is difficult:
    Its operatic moans
A touch too grand.

Snow softens every edge
    That hard wind hones.
The black waves scare
    The shivering stones.
Pinched faces, little man,
    And bones,
The sheep are growing
    Overcoats of frost.
They aren't alone –

The waves are also cold
    Though never lost,
Unlike those creatures
    Learning to their cost
That snow is of a mind
    To lay them low,
As everyone who meets it
    Comes to know.
Here. Hold my hand.

The Light Programme

I ask if he can linger longer
(Our kitchen Nelson Eddy,
Our hallway Richard Tauber)
But no – as Jim Reeves
Almost sang – he has to go,
Though not before a final
Cod and chips, with salt
And vinga-vonga.

Lost Things

But if the dead return for one last look around
the house they used to own way back, and, somewhat stern,
brush past you without a sound, leaving you alone,
stupid in the hallway, let that moment go
then offer them a seat, or take them into all
the rooms they used to know, however incomplete.
How out of place they'll seem – their tissue-paper crowns,
their Sunday best – prepared for fun or walking in a dream.
Ignore their frowns. Remember they are scared.
Let them linger for a while. Ask if they are well.
Should they appreciate your choices, nod and smile.
Suggest they tell their stories. Stay up late;
and when they cry or swear, attempt to comprehend
the loss of dining chairs, of books, of threadbare
light they couldn't mend, of a sleepy cat on the stairs,
of a working train-set half-built in the attic,
of a black & white TV that hasn't failed them yet,
of a melodramatic print of the sea,
of crockery, of drawers and cupboards stuffed with screws
and rawlplugs and fuses and rubber bands – vast stores
of things they didn't use, of things that no one uses
any more, lost things they're sure they left . . . but where?
If only they knew how everything vanished, like rings
from off their fingers . . . There – those fingers,
touching you.

We Lived Here

not so far from narwhals! mink! & who knew
    crex crex! Keeley Hawes! the common hen!
around the corner from the sweetshop's drinks
    & papers! wrapping paper! string! & other
useful things we lived with iffy drains
    & plaster crumbling to the touch
& oscillating infants off on daylong trips
    to Birdworld's fowl/The Sea Life Centre's fish
we lived here with *cephalanthera longifolia*!
    Jump in! a cupboard full of shoes
in which our high & mighty moggy curled
    here we lived with late-night boozers!
bugs! some butterflies! I could go on
        I might / might not

O years & years before your own year dot
    with rain & snow or when it shone
with DIYers! wind-up merchants! losers!
    a short walk through the world
where yelps & growls outdid most zoos
    across the street from nothing holier
than Andy's skylight & satellite dish
    & the doughnut smell! with skips
& ladders! loft extensions that much
    closer to the clouds' low aeroplanes
we lived here! your sister me your mother
    calling from the pansies! pinks!
a California lilac tree! then
        so did you

Happly Ever After

for Kate

We bellow from the roaf toaps homemade *rooftops*
flags and baners stripy scarfs aLoft
one day in April clamber once apon a time
up Lamposts qwike as pigs despite the cowsuls *council's*
ante vandle paint the mums the yape kids *yappy*
with yape dogs out from the darke the oaps
un yust to lite returnd like Laserus to find *unused*
there streets and houses good again
we point at jumbos wow WOW taxis neenors *fire engines*
growl at purrgos bumbl throw puddls *Peugeots*
oh NO but what of that then sun are selvs
on every levl serfis call in sik to darnce
the darncis Lernt all turm in darncicaltey *Dansicality*
lak of rithum no exgus we tuch   sea *excuse*
here   smel   tast   no complikashun
nuthing to prpel the afternone towords
anuther evning sharp with smoke we sing
all day ower voicies scuft and gloreus
ower scarfs are not for ceping warm
ower baners nither liy nor beg who
nose what we can see from here
bloons and bunting bilbords botls bricks
rose of houses benchis brigis steepuls *bridges*
woshing lines the tooker tooker pilot *helicopter*
smiling down on us ARE MEN

are men to that

99 Poems

i.m.

A face that, though in shadow, still appears
A graceful Child, his father's joy!
A ship-wrack on his bed, night being past
Abandoned by day in a pinkish lounge, his final
ahv naebawdy
'Allas!' quaþ he, 'now me is wo
Almost as true as his kindness, I'll say, almost as true as his
    laughter, his labored jokes
Ane faiding flour, away as wind it weiris
Angled to face each other
Are you to leave like this

Before you say
Below this faultless Stone, is laid
Bid mountain-light attend your bower
Brimmer Street irregular! Father's barbarous dress-sword

Carriages, clergymen, unsmiling faces, delicate hands
Cold rivers, colder seas, alas

Death's oompah band

'E weren't no bloomin' 'ero, all 'e did was live an' die
Empire State patrician

Fare-thee-well, o glaikit man
Farewel, more lov'd than any I recal
Father! how soon this night o'er-brims the trees
Fog after dusk, murmuring small requests
Fold the sky in half, shake out the stars

For he is affraid
fus ting dat crazy clack

Go, finde a Store of Tears among the Clouds
God of all things, all things rain and air, all flying things

He gave his Checks – the Whistle blew
He Rambld Ere The Mornings Dews Could Flee
He visited the loft, not long before
He was withouten any peere
He woke again last night, and cried
Here he sat, his face o'ershadowed
Here rests a gentle Man, whose modest Heart
Here shall he rest for evermo
His dreaming eyes, his brow in touch
His hat still on its peg. His shoes lined up
His watch-face like a skating rink
How still the moon-blanch'd sea
'How's the Humber? How's the wife? Do you remember Lilian?'

I dreamed you stood alone, in No Man's Land
I have seen Him in a meagre light
I sought, ô grassie mountaines, thy constant fellowship
I THOUGHT of Thee, unfathomable one
I took no part
Icy nim-air, a barn done Dinner Street
If Death, growne wearie of his warres
Il laisse tomber son modelling knife, *tant pis, tant pis*

Lately, I have seen the fellow with his pockets inside out
Lethean foam-flowers rise from the sewers
Like as a winde that fadeth ere blacke night
Lost in the pea-drills behind our house
LOVE NAILS   TriBeCa Nails   (too much

May his comfy shoes, O Lord
Mr Chips, Bulk Catering
My dreams of thee! How soon the morning comes!
My father had heard tell
My father picked up a stone
My latest thoughts return to thee

[. . .] nis þer no niȝte
Niver say tha'rt frit o' me
No murmur stirs your room, tonight, no voices call below
No nothin kin explain it, yes indeedy
No winde there blew, the skie was bare of anie bird

O thou whose falt'ring hand the waters tune
O turn thy Waters through my Heart
Oh, sweet was the rain as it fell on Swiss Cottage
Once my Lamentation was an envied horror

Plip plop plip

Sisyphus, your heart
Snow in the branches, where birds perch still as graves
Stars observe, with their flat blank eyes
Sythen in that spote hit fro me sprange

There was a crappy bookstore smell, *jeez*. Old guys
The fields of snow did breathe
The laundromat is crowded. Every ghost
The sea it was brazen and icy
The Show'r come down on Tory and Whig, Dust gone to Mud
The stairs became more difficult
Thy Exile from this World, deare Friend
Thy Publick Virtue, Father, all attest
'Tis three years since, his grave is bare

Uh-oh

Vnmesurable greiff, Alas! how straunge is this
Voices on the wireless

We are becoming
Weepe with me, to night, all hope is over-come
Well, then! Let no man disapprove
When first your slender breath
When the evenèn wind do blow vrom zight
Where rootless poppies lie
Who could not stay a while

Yf all my wordes were raine upon thy grave
Yonder
You could not face me, then
You could not speak, nor even smile, before you turned
You cupped one hand to catch the crumbs
Your hands

CB *editions*

Fergus Allen *Before Troy*
Guillaume Apollinaire *The Little Auto*
(translated by Beverley Bie Brahic)
Jonathan Barrow *The Queue*
Beverley Bie Brahic *White Sheets*
Andrzej Bursa *Killing Auntie and Other Work*
(translated by Wiesiek Powaga)
Nancy Gaffield *Tokaido Road*
Joaquín Giannuzzi *A Complicated Mammal*
(translated by Richard Gwyn)
Stefan Grabiński *In Sarah's House*
(translated by Wiesiek Powaga)
Gert Hofmann *Lichtenberg & The Little Flower Girl*
(translated by Michael Hofmann)
Erik Houston *The White Room*
Gabriel Josipovici *Only Joking*
David Markson *This Is Not a Novel*
Miha Mazzini *The German Lottery*
(translated by Urska Zupanec)
J. O. Morgan *Natural Mechanical*
J. O. Morgan *Long Cuts*
D. Nurkse *Voices over Water*
Francis Ponge *Unfinished Ode to Mud*
(translated by Beverley Bie Brahic)
Christopher Reid *The Song of Lunch*
Jack Robinson *Days and Nights in W12*
Nicky Singer *Knight Crew*
Elise Valmorbida *The TV President*
Dai Vaughan *Sister of the artist*
Jennie Walker *24 for 3*
Marjorie Ann Watts *Are they funny, are they dead?*

---

www.cbeditions.com